Man is never at peace until
he is at one with his Creator.
No matter how far you think
you have fallen and how
unhappy you are,

Just open your heart to God
and He will give you peace.

MY PEACE I GIVE YOU

Merciful Jesus we believe in You
and we trust in You,
Come to the aid of our weakness
and our incapacity,
Grant that we may be able to make you
known and loved by all,
And that confident in the immensity
of Your love
we may be able to combat the evil
that is in us,
and in all the world for Your glory
and our salvation.
Amen

Divine Mercy Publications

TALK TO ME, I AM YOUR GOD

A HANDBOOK FOR
THE SACRAMENT
OF CONFESSION

Val Conlon

Divine Mercy Publications
Maryville, Skerries, Co. Dublin, Ireland
Tel: 00 353 1 8491458 Fax: 00 353 1 8492466
Email: info@divinemercy.org

Springtime Productions USA
5124 Karen Dr,
Fort Worth , TX 76180, USA
Tel: 682-557-3976

Canadian Divine Mercy Distribution Centre
PO Box 812
Smiths Fall, ON, K7A 4W7, Canada
Tel: 613-205-1540 / 800-461-9254

www.divinemercy.org
Divine Mercy in Action - www.hudt.org

ISBN 1-1872276-87-3 Printed in Ireland

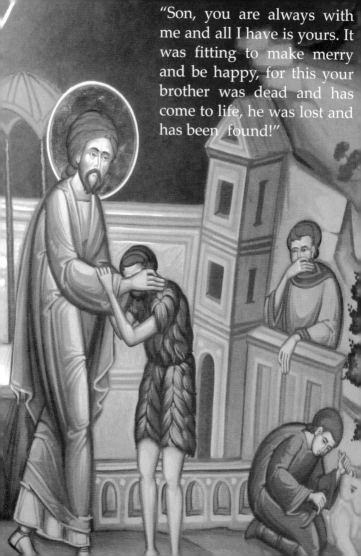

"Son, you are always with me and all I have is yours. It was fitting to make merry and be happy, for this your brother was dead and has come to life, he was lost and has been found!"

We thank Jesus
for having called us to live this
particular service to His Church
and we ask for all who serve Him
the gift of true faith.

Divine Mercy Publications

TABLE OF CONTENTS

*"If we say we have no sin
we deceive ourselves
and the truth is not in us"* ...

(1 John 1:8)

yet...

*"It is a beautiful thought,
my children,
that we have a Sacrament
which heals the wounds of our soul! "*

(Saint John Vianney)

Understanding Sin and the Mystery of Reconciliation

"I fail the good I want to do and I practice the bad that I do not want to practice. But if I do what I have no desire to do, then I am no longer doing it myself, but rather sin that makes itself a home in me" (Romans 7:19-20).

It is to wash away the sin that makes a home in us that Jesus was born, made man, was crucified, died and came back to life, for only the mercy and the grace of God can restore us to fullness as true children of God.

The first thing that we all need to do is admit the truth that we are sinners. *"If we say we have no sin we deceive ourselves and the truth is not in us"* (1 John 1:8).

What is written in Sacred Scripture is true for all of us, no matter how much we may think we are good, to different degrees we slip back into sin too frequently.

Trying to absolve ourselves by blurring the boundaries of morality or ignoring the sin won't make the consequences go away. The results of sin can cause grief and suffering, both in mind and in body, there is always an unconscious sense of guilt and uneasiness that sometimes leads to a despair that we may not even understand. Letting sin make a home in us, trying to justify a sin to ourselves will only damage more and more our relationship with God. We will then try to find new ways to justify other sins and end up denying everything that reminds us of the real truth. The mask of pretence that we use in our lives we may use to hide from the world, but nothing can hide the real person from the one who created us.

As St. Augustine pointed out that in failing to acknowledge our sins, *"I only hide them from myself, but not from You, O Lord!"*.

It is said that we only begin our life as Christians when our spiritual eyes are awakened to the constant battle between good and evil, not only without, but also within. Being aware - this is the first step we must take in preparing ourselves for discerning and choosing the right path: a path where life in Christ can take place within us, removing all sin and even more, the consequence of sin.

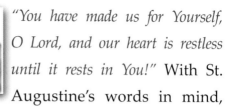 *"You have made us for Yourself, O Lord, and our heart is restless until it rests in You!"* With St. Augustine's words in mind, we need to aknowledge the sin within us as a reality to be addressed and in doing this, we need to put all our trust in God's Merciful and forgiving Love: for God's Mercy and Love is real and ever present, always there waiting for us.

The only way to give ourselves peace of mind in this life, which includes hope of achieving eternal life, is full communion with God through the sacraments, which He has given to us for that purpose. We are all created for this mystical rest in the Heart of God and nothing has the power to separate us from His Ocean of Mercy:

"Who shall separate us from the love of Christ? Shall tribulation, distress, persecution, hunger, nakedness, danger...the sword?

For I am sure that neither death, nor life, nor angels, nor principalities, nor things present, nor things to come, nor power, nor height, nor depth, nor any other creature will be able to separate us from the love of God, which is in Christ Our Lord" (Romans 8:35-39).

Sin is a matter of life and death, in fact a matter of eternal life and eternal death and given that we are all sinners, God gave us a set of rules, in fact they are more than rules, they are Commandments: (Book of Exodus Ch. 20):

I am the Lord your God: you shall not have strange Gods before me.

 *You shall not take the name of the Lord your God in vain.*

Remember to keep holy the Lord's Day.

Honour your father and your mother.

You shall not kill.

You shall not commit adultery.

You shall not steal.

You shall not bear false witness against your neighbour.

You shall not covet your neighbour's wife.

You shall not covet your neighbour's goods.

These commandments cover all the major sins (mortal) and many groups of lesser sins (venial). But notice that almost all of these Ten Commandments are in the negative sense in that they tell us what not to do. So to compliment these, in the New Testament, Jesus gave us with His amazing Sermon on the Mount, a set of new guidelines on how to live and went even further by letting us know  what the rewards would be for following His teachings. This great list is known as the eight beatitudes (from the Latin word *"blessed"*), referring to blessings in relation to finding true happiness. They are found in the Gospel of St. Matthew (Ch. 5).

Eight Beatitudes

Happy are the poor in spirit for theirs is the Kingdom of Heaven.

Happy are those who mourn for they shall be comforted.

Happy are the meek for they shall inherit the earth.

Happy are those who hunger and thirst for justice, for they shall be satisfied.

Happy are the merciful for they shall obtain mercy.

Happy are the pure of heart for they shall see God.

Happy are the peacemakers for they shall be called children of God.

Happy are those who are persecuted for the Kingdom of Heaven belongs to them.

In these beatitudes Jesus offers us a lifestyle different from the ways of the world. It is an inverted perspective on things. It is aimed at the majority, those who are unfortunate and are struggling in life, he is comforting them by saying it is not about this world it is about the next, and that success and riches in this life mean nothing, He means you must be meek and humble to inherit the Kingdom of God, but this does not preclude the successful who believe in God and relate their success to prayer and belief in God. It goes without saying that if the successful are meek and humble they too will also inherit the Kingdom. God died for all Mankind, rich, poor, healthy, disabled, all.

Today the whole world is being looked at from a human perspective, and many successful people believe their success comes from God. Just look at how many successful athletes and footballers bless themselves before and after an event they are involved in. We can only make sense of God's words if we have faith and believe and follow Jesus as our guide and our light no matter what our station in life is.

Christian morality is based quite simply on

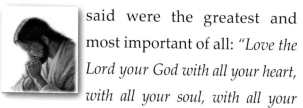 said were the greatest and most important of all: *"Love the Lord your God with all your heart, with all your soul, with all your mind and with all your strength"* and *"love your neighbour as you love yourself"*

By striving to follow all these, we begin to move in the right direction and even if we are to fall again, *"let us then approach the throne of grace with confidence, so that we may receive Mercy and find Grace to help us in our time of need."*(*Heb 4:16*)

The Sacrament of Reconciliation (Confession)

Return to the Lord, your God, for he is gracious and merciful, slow to anger and abounding in steadfast love. (*Joel 2:12-13*)

$\mathcal{O}$nce we admit to ourselves the truth and accept that we have sinned, help is close at hand because *"if we confess our sins, he is faithful and just, and will forgive our sins and cleanse us from unrighteousness" (1 John 1:9).*

Our attitudes don't change overnight because we are complex human beings, with deep-rooted desires, being self centred, selfish, always acquiring possessions and searching for sensual fulfilment. It is a constant battle but within each of us dwells the Spirit of God to help us when we fall, time after time and God is there to help us to try to live a good life and to avoid the many daily temptations.

You must remember that reconciliation is one

of the seven sacraments of Jesus and Jesus Christ holds our hand as you confess to almighty God during this sacrament. So there is nothing to be afraid of. This grace of forgiveness, peace and healing comes directly from God through Jesus Christ so that the sinner is absolutely and completely forgiven of all their sins.

Defeating sin is not an easy process for anyone. Though we love God and want to please Him, we are sinful people, living in a world full of temptations. We will fall into sin, again and again, time after time but we should never let this weakness depress us.

In the words of St. Francis de Sales, *"Don't be anxious to condemn yourself every time you fall. Instead, patiently, pick yourself up and start again. Why are you surprised when the weak turns out to be weak and the frail, frail, or when you turn out to be sinful?* *When you fall, be gentle with yourself. Lift yourself up gently, accept your failure without wallowing in your weakness. Admit your guilt in God's sight, then with good heart, with courage and confidence in His mercy, start over again."*

We can repent, receive forgiveness and pray that with Jesus' help, we will try to do better the next time. This process of sinning and repentance will continue throughout our earthly life, but we will slowly, through God's grace, begin to overcome certain areas in our lives that cause us to sin.

There are certain things that help us,

firstly, our conscience. In most of us, this is a "safety valve" that guides us to do what is right even when we have already done something wrong. Secondly, sorrow, saying sorry is often the hardest thing, but really meaning it and seeking forgiveness, this along with our conscience is our ever-open doorway to the Sacrament of Reconciliation. *To have a delicate conscience is to possess a great gift.*

The Sacrament of Reconciliation is also a process of recognition: firstly, that we are sinners; secondly, that only God can forgive sins; thirdly, that we want to accept God's gift of forgiveness and fourthly, that with a contrite heart, we will endeavour to change our sinful ways, no matter how hard the task may seem.

Many may have fears about going to Confession but the teaching of the Catholic Church states that, *"There is no*

sin so great that God cannot forgive, provided that the repentance is sincere and honest". (CCC 982)

Look at the great Saints Peter and Paul, the two pillars of the Church: St Peter denied Christ three times and St. Paul before his conversion, openly persecuted Christians and approved of the murder of St. Stephen. But their sin did not prevail, for they both repented, they turned to God, they recognized Him as the source of all Life and Mercy and they received the redeeming grace that saved them.

In contrast, Judas was lost by not repenting. Repenting would have brought him forgiveness and peace. True remorse would have brought him to the foot of the Cross, in the presence of the One who is Mercy and Love. Judas' incomplete remorse brought him to despair.

Choosing hope, Peter runs to the empty tomb and believes. Choosing despair, Judas gives back the price of betrayal and runs to put an end to his life... And the Gospels are full of accounts of Jesus' forgiveness, including the woman caught in the act of adultery or Jesus forgiving those who put Him to death on the cross. The lives of the Saints are another endless source of inspiration regarding forgiveness and healing through the Sacrament of Confession.

The question most often asked  especially from those from different Christian backgrounds is, "Why must I confess my sins to a Priest?" Jesus gave the apostles authority on earth to forgive sins. The Gospel of St. John records the following lesson that Jesus taught his disciples: *Jesus came and stood among them. He said to them, "Peace be with you", and showed them His hands and side. The disciples were filled with joy when they saw the Lord and He said to them again, "Peace be with you, as the Father sent me, so I am sending you". After this He breathed on them and said: "Receive the Holy Spirit. For those whose sins you forgive, they are forgiven...for those whose sins you shall retain they are retained "* (20:19-22)

The priest therefore is the sign and the

instrument of God's merciful love for the sinner and is the designated servant of God's forgiveness. One of the greatest Fathers of the early Church, St. John Chrysostom encourages us to *"enter into the Church and wash away your sins. For this is a hospital for sinners and not a court of law."*

Let us not fear then to approach this Mystery, for it is not judgement that awaits us in this Holy Sacrament, but healing and peace.

Another point often raised even by Catholics is, "My sins are always the same each time I go to Confession". This is true, because we are always falling into sin and many of our sins, especially the venial sins, will be the same and repetitive. In answer to this, Pope Benedict XVI had this to say:

"It is true, our sins are always the same, but we clean our homes, our rooms at least once a week, even if the dirt is always the same in order to live in cleanliness, in order to start again. Otherwise, the dirt might not be seen, but it builds up again".

So then, don't worry about confessing the same thing again, think of it in the same way as cleaning your home, only this time you are cleansing your soul.

Before celebrating the Sacrament of Reconciliation, we must first pray and examine our own conscience. We can get into the habit of doing this by reviewing each night, before going to bed, our actions and words of the day just passed, then praying to the Lord for help, to help us defeat our faults and failings. When we examine our conscience before going to confession, we should not be disheartened by the fact that we are always sinning.

God understands our human failings which come about through His granting us free will, which is so important for us, to be able to live as individuals in God's overall plan for the human race.

This covenant of "Free Will" is what makes us human and often influences us to do things arrogantly in our own way, living to

our own rules, but often we know we are wrong, but we don't allow ourselves to dwell on it.

We need to be more aware that our decisions in life and our anxieties and fears should always be guided by our faith.

But remember each time we attend Mass, we confess all the small wrongs we have done in the Penitential Rite and with the priest we ask for mercy for these wrongs.

The Sacrament of Reconciliation is of course a one to one with God. It can be in a confessional box, behind a screen, or more and more today, a face to face talk with a priest. After you have confessed your sins, you listen to the priest's advice which should be

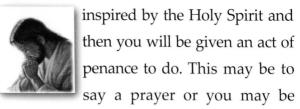 inspired by the Holy Spirit and then you will be given an act of penance to do. This may be to say a prayer or you may be asked to perform a good deed or act of charity. The act of penance is a sign of our sorrow for offending God and is part of the healing process.

At the end of the celebration of the sacrament, Christ uses the priest for the channel of His love and mercy to flow, which will absolve us of our sins: "… *May God give you pardon and peace and I absolve you from your sins, in the name of the Father, and of the Son, and of the Holy Spirit*"; after accepting God's forgiveness, we should then be filled with joy as we are cleansed and feel peace in our hearts again.

It is also good from time to
time to reflect on the good
things that we do in our life
because most people do far
more good than bad.

Remember every time we forgive someone, every time we show compassion to a
suffering person, every time we put others
first, every word spoken and action taken
to promote a just world, means we are
following in the footsteps of Jesus Christ.

POPE JOHN PAUL II ON CONFESSION

"TO SPEAK OF RECONCILIATION
AND PENANCE IS FOR THE MEN
AND WOMEN OF OUR TIME AN
INVITATION TO REDISCOVER THE
VERY WORDS WITH WHICH OUR
SAVIOUR AND TEACHER
JESUS CHRIST
BEGAN HIS PREACHING:

" REPENT "

☩ ☩ ☩ ☩ ☩ ☩

" REPENT "

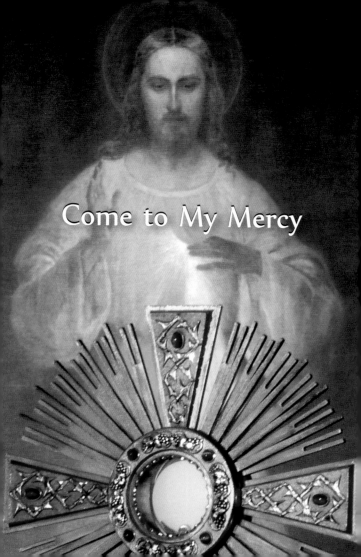

Come to My Mercy

"Go to your confessor; open your heart to him; display to him all the recesses of your soul; take the advice that he will give you with the utmost humility and simplicity.

For God, Who has an infinite love for obedience, frequently renders profitable the counsels we take from others, but especially from those who are the guides of our souls."

St. Francis de Sales

Steps on the Road to
a Good Confession

With living life in the "fast lane" and with so much information trying to get his attention, the modern man finds it difficult to slow down, to stop and in silence, to contemplate, to meditate and to ask the important questions of life.

One thing that we might not realise is that in the history of humankind, many things have changed but on a human level things change very little.

There is no doubt that in the history of the world, science and technical advancements have transformed the world into a different place altogether; but humankind as a whole and each one of us as individuals face the same timeless questions about life, death, about our soul and our purpose in life.

So it comes as no surprise to find out that in approaching the Mystery and Sacrament of

Confession in the Church, nothing has really changed since the very beginning of the Church.

We look today at the spiritual advice from Fathers of the Early Church, like St. John Chrysostom in the 5th century and from theologians like St. Thomas Aquinas in the 13th century, or from the Saints of the 20th century like St. Faustina, Padre Pio or St. John Paul II and they are all as valid and profound in understanding the human soul as they were one hundred years ago, seven hundred years ago or fifteen hundred years ago.

But many people today, wanting to break away from the discipline and dignity that religion requires and from a personal relationship with their Creator, now seek mental and emotional counselling, psycho-analysis and psychotherapy as forms of dealing with the burdens of modern living.

The fact is that even the most intellectual or

the ones that totally reject God and the notion that there is a forgiving Father awaiting the return of the prodigal son, still feel the need to share the burden of their inner guilt with someone. Is this not a sure sign that they are searching for something more?

There is a great debate, even in scientific circles about how effective these methods are; but one thing that is missing in all of these searchings for peace of mind is the **forgiveness factor**, the feeling and peace that comes with knowing that you have been forgiven for your wrongdoing, the supernatural grace of knowing that you can be at one with your Creator again and the loving embrace and the reassuring words:

"For this son of mine was dead and is alive again; he was lost and now is found."

CONFESSION
THE NECESSARY STEPS FOR A
GOOD CONFESSION

"The person who knows how to acknowledge the truth of guilt, and asks Christ for forgiveness, enhances his own human dignity and manifests spiritual greatness. Because of Christ's love and mercy, there is no sin that is too great to be forgiven; there is no sinner who will be rejected. Every person who repents will be received by Jesus Christ with forgiveness and immense love." (St. Pope John Paul II)

These are the words of a great Apostle of God's Mercy, St. Pope John Paul II: *"No sin too great to be forgiven and no sinner who will be rejected..."* With this in mind, we should have great hope when we prepare ourselves for a good confession.

It helps a lot to start by praying earnestly to God and Our Lady, the Angels and Saints, asking for divine light.

The first step we have to take is a careful

Examination of Conscience: (see page 56).
Here, we have to be sincere and true to ourselves, reflecting upon all our failures, in deeds, words, thoughts and omissions.

The second step is
Sincere sorrow for sin:
This is the most essential condition in order to obtain God's forgiveness. Without true contrition, there is no pardoning. The prodigal son comes back to the Father with a humble heart and full of remorse: *"Father, I have sinned against heaven and against you!"*

The third step is
A firm resolution to sin no more:
To avoid, with God's grace, sin and the occasion of sin. This third step is very much linked with the previous one, for the two together will play such an important part in obtaining the Mercy of God.

The fourth step is

Confession to a priest:
The priest is seen as the instrument of God's Merciful Love. Remember that it is not judgement awaiting us in this Sacrament but healing and the peace of mind we lost through sinning.

The fifth step is
Reconciliation with God:
Our acceptance of penance in reparation for the offence or offences against God for sins we have committed. The sin is then forgiven and this is the debt we have to pay.

When preparing for Confession, we should be convinced that our eternal welfare depends on this Sacrament and on the way we approach it.

Many saints have said that we should prepare for each Confession, with great trust and sincerity as if it were to be our last.

The **Confession** itself should be made **openly** and **sincerely**, with a **humble heart** and in a **complete** manner, that is, telling each mortal sin committed since our last Confession.

It is very important to know that **sorrow** for the sins committed must be **interior**, coming from the heart, must be in the heart and not on the lips.

True sorrow is a grace received from God when we decide to reject anything that offends Him. To obtain this supernatural grace, we think of His infinite goodness and Mercy, keeping in mind the sacrifice of Our Lord on the Cross and the reward of Eternal Life.

The contrition (sorrow) has to be **sincere**, and come from the heart, meaning that we must detest our sins more than anything else and the sorrow must extend to every mortal sin committed since our last Confession.

Then, the resolution to avoid sin must be

firm, for there must be a strong determination to avoid all mortal sin and to adopt all the necessary means and measures to avoid sin in the future.

The resolution has also to be **long lasting**, not just a resolution on the day, but a firm determination to reject and stay away from anything that would offend God again.

Lastly, **accepting the penance** with a contrite heart is necessary in order to restore the divine order and the penance has to be performed as soon as possible;

If this is not possible to be fulfilled before going to Holy Communion, it has to be done before the next Confession, otherwise the Sacrament is incomplete (not invalidated, but still incomplete).

Mortal Sin is to choose deliberately - that is, both knowing it and willing it - something gravely contrary to the divine law and to the ultimate end of man. Mortal sin destroys in us the charity without which eternal beatitude is impossible. Unrepented, it brings eternal death. (C.C.C. # 1874)

Venial Sin without being strictly necessary to confess, confessing is nevertheless strongly recommended by the Church. Indeed, regular confession of our venial sins helps us form our conscience and fight against evil tendencies.

By receiving more frequently the gift of the Father's mercy, we are spurred to be merciful as He is merciful. (C.C.C. # 1458)

Confession heals,
confession justifies,
confession grants pardon
of sin,

hope for the future
comes from
a good confession,

in confession
there is healing
and a mercy.

MY PEACE I GIVE YOU

The greatest quest in life
has always been
the search for peace
and many have travelled far and wide
in search of it.

But peace is given by God
to man and is available everywhere.

The path to peace is a direct line
from God to man.

It is the oneness of divinity
and humanity.

see Jeremiah 29:13

Did you know that...

We can say with all confidence that there are very few people who lived upon this earth who understood the importance of Confession better that Padre Pio.

Many Saints had a deep understanding of the mysteries and graces of the Sacrament of Reconciliation, but among other super-natural gifts, a special gift was given to Padre Pio: reading the souls of penitents.

Countless are the cases where the "Martyr of the Confessional", as Padre Pio was called, read the souls of people like an open book.

Sins forgotten, omitted or hidden were brought to light, with an invitation from Padre Pio to the penitent to come back to God with a heart full of love and contrition.

For as long as 50 years, sometimes for 12 hours a day, Padre Pio listened to confessions, as people from all over the world came to him, seeking to become his spiritual sons and daughters. His advice and his understanding of the depths of the human soul saved many and converted many.

Why were people looking to find God in his confessional? Pope Paul VI gives us the answer: *"Was it because he was a philosopher, because he was wise, because he had great means at his disposal? No - it was because he said Mass humbly, heard confessions from morning till night and was - a hard thing to say - a representative of Our Lord, sealed with His very wounds. He was a man of prayer and suffering"*

Examination of

Conscience

"Be still and know that I am God"

"Turn inward, and in everything you do, see God as your witness"

(St. Augustine)

While most people will agree that without a good examination of conscience there can be no valid confession, this practice of "turning inward, with God as our witness" should in fact become a daily practice in our life: a time set aside, a time of holy silence when one can look back and think of the day that has just passed by.

This daily examination of conscience should be part of our prayer life, because the two go and grow in fact together and this is how one's spiritual life develops and after a while, it bears much fruit.

If we eliminate by negligence these spiritual practices out of our daily life, the "noise" and the "busyness" around us will eventually numb this voice of conscience in our heart; this is why a nightly examination of conscience is an important

 form of prayer and at the same time, it is a great way of developing that special spiritual openness that will allow us to recognise and respond positively to God's Will in our lives.

St. Ignatius of Loyola promoted a simple way of examining one's conscience on a daily basis as part of the evening's prayers. The time set apart for this can and will vary as there is no limit to the time that someone wants to spend in this inner communion with God.

DAILY GENERAL EXAMINATION OF CONSCIENCE AS A FORM OF PRAYER

St. Ignatius

1. Give thanks to God Our Lord for favours received.

2. Ask for the grace to know your sins.

3. Examine how you have lived this day.

4. Ask forgiveness for any faults.

5. Resolve to amend them with the grace of God.

As you can see, there are no prescribed prayers. In the holy silence of your own heart, this inner conversation with God has to come also from the heart. "With God alone as your witness", you are now the judge of your own actions and thoughts, of your omissions and failures. It is in your power now to give thanks, to ask for grace, to examine your life, to ask forgiveness and to resolve to amend any failure. This daily examination will pave your way back to God and the healing power of the great sacraments of Confession and Holy Communion will restore the peace and balance in your life. These five steps will help you grow each day until one day, God's will and yours will become one.

EXAMINATION OF CONSCIENCE BEFORE GOING TO CONFESSION

The following examination of conscience is adapted from the Rite of Penance of the Catholic Church and is a simplified version that in fact only opens a door, inviting us to look deeper into our soul, searching for answers to any questions that our conscience might bring up. A spiritual director (a priest that gets to know the penitent after a period of time) is the right person to discuss any issues regarding one's doubts and scruples. (Begin by praying to God for His Grace and His Divine Light; there are many helpful prayers on page 64, but you should primarily try to use your own words, from your heart)

Some preliminary questions

Am I willing to look at the Good and Evil in my life and to call them by their proper names?

Am I sincere in wanting to start a new life and friendship with God by this confession? Did I forget or deliberately conceal past

serious sins in my last confession?
Have I ever received Holy Communion while in a state of mortal sin?

Did I make an honest effort to repair any damage done to others? Did I sincerely do the penance I was given at my last confession and do my best in trying to lead a better life?

Questions related to the greatest commandment: to love the Lord your God with your whole heart.

Do I love God the Father above all else, obeying His Commandments as He wished and putting His Will before mine in all that I do?

Is my faith in God strong and sure? Have I done my best to learn more about my faith and the teachings of the Church? Have I shown real strength of purpose in professing my faith both in public and private?

Do I pray daily and with real meaning, offering all my troubles, joys and thanks to God? Do I ask God's help in times of temptation and do I thank Him for all favours and blessings in my life?

Am I careful not to take the Lord's name in vain or that of His Blessed Mother? Did I show disrespect to the Church, Sacraments, Saints, holy things?

Have I intentionally missed Mass on Sundays or on holy days of obligation or caused others to do so also?

Have I received at least annual confession and communion during Easter?

Do I place more meaning on material things, superstition or occult practices than God? Are there any "false gods" ruling my life?

Questions related to the commandment of a right love of self and the love of neighbour: "You shall love your neighbour as yourself"

Am I doing my best to improve my spiritual life, through prayer, confession, receiving the holy Sacraments of the Church? Am I growing in my spiritual life? Have I tried to control any excesses or selfishness in my behaviour? Have I always tried to show respect to others?

Have I used all the gifts God has given me fully and for the good of others?

Have I done unto others as I would have others do unto me?

Have I tried to bring happiness into my home by showing patience, love and respect for all the members of my family? Have I been a good parent in all my familial duties and tried to lead by example?

Have I been always faithful to my spouse, both in my heart and with others?

Do I treat everyone equally and share with the less fortunate? Are there many or any works of Mercy towards the less fortunate that I can show God?

Do I try to be a good apostle for the church, through prayer, charitable works and spreading the word of God when I can?

Have I tried to be a good citizen in my community, thinking of others and promoting harmony and justice?

Have I dealt honestly in my work or profession with others, showing fairness with employees and business contacts?

Have I shown respect for all legal aspects of business?

Do I abuse any position of authority I may hold for my own good?

Have I shown violence towards others either physically, materially or by damaging anyone's reputation or honour? Have I held a grudge, quarrelled, been insulting or failed to prove another's innocence when I could have, because it was not to my benefit?

Have I endangered the sacred gift of life by advising, encouraging or procuring an abortion?

Have I been chaste in mind and body and done my best to act in a pure manner in my daily life?

Have I tried always to be fair and tell the truth and to avoid hurting others through lies, deceit, rash judgement or violation of a secret?

Have I stolen from others, or damaged property failing to make good the loss?

Have I been quick to forgive any injury to myself in the name of peace and love of God?

OUR PURPOSE OF AMENDMENT

To be truly sorry for one's sins, we, as Christians, must resolve not only to avoid sin but also strive to advance spiritually by praying more and doing more for others and the church.

Examples of personal efforts
that will lead to spiritual growth:

- Daily examination of one's conscience

- Take a scriptural reading and reflect on it for a few minutes each day. Try to apply it to your own life.

- Choose a good Christian book to study for half an hour once a week.

- Aspire to be more disciplined in your work and study.

- Resolve to try to get to know more about the people you work and socialise with.

- Perform one selfless act each day, out of pure love of God.

- Do something for those in need at least once a week.

- Make an effort to get Mass one extra day per week.

- Receive confession monthly.

- Show compassion for and try to comfort those with problems or in distress.

Prayers

before

Confession

AN ACT OF CONTRITION
BEFORE CONFESSION

O my God, I am heartily sorry for having offended You, and I detest all my sins because of Your just punishments, but most of all because they offend You, my God, Who are all-good and deserving of all my love.

I firmly resolve, with the help of Your grace, to confess all my sins, to do my penance, to sin no more and to avoid occasions of sin.

Amen.

A PRAYER
BEFORE CONFESSION

My Lord and my God, I am sorry for all my sins with all my heart. In choosing to do wrong and failing to do good, I have sinned against You whom I should love above all things.

With your help, I firmly intend to confess all my sins, to do penance, to sin no more, and to avoid whatever leads me to sin.

My Lord and my God, who suffered and died for us, have mercy on me.

Amen.

CONFITEOR

The Confiteor (from the latin word I Confess) is a penitential prayer acknowledging our sins and seeking God's mercy and forgiveness.

Penitential Prayers have been part of Christian Tradition from the beginning. The Confiteor was traditionally recited while striking the breast, as a sign of penitence and humility.

The prayer below is the traditional form of the prayer. The Confiteor we use at the beginning of the Mass is a shortened version of the traditional one.

I confess to almighty God, to blessed Mary ever Virgin, to blessed Michael the Archangel, to blessed John the Baptist, to the holy Apostles Peter and Paul, and to all the saints, that I have sinned exceedingly in thought, word and deed, through my fault, through my fault, through my most grievous fault.

Therefore, I beseech blessed Mary ever Virgin, blessed Michael the Archangel, blessed John the Baptist, the holy Apostles Peter and Paul, and all the saints, to pray for me to the Lord our God. Amen.

CONFITEOR

I confess to almighty God and to you, my brothers and sisters, that I have greatly sinned in my thoughts and in my words, in what I have done and in what I have failed to do, through my fault, through my fault, through my most grievous fault; therefore I ask blessed Mary ever-Virgin, all the Angels and Saints, and you, my brothers and sisters, to pray for me to the Lord our God.

Amen.

ANOTHER SIMPLE PRAYER
BEFORE CONFESSION

*D*ear Jesus, help me to make a good Confession,

Help me to know my sins,

Help me to be sorry for them,

Help me to make up my mind not to sin again.

Have mercy on me O Lord, and forgive me.

Mary my Mother, pray for me.

Amen.

PRAYER FOR ENLIGHTENMENT BEFORE CONFESSION

Come Holy Spirit into my soul and enlighten my mind that I may know the sins I have to confess, and grant me Your grace to confess them fully, humbly and with a contrite heart. Help me to firmly resolve not to commit them again.

O Blessed Virgin, my Mother and the Mother of my Redeemer, mirror of innocence and sanctity, refuge of penitent sinners, intercede for me through the Passion of Your Son, that I may obtain the grace to make a good confession.

All you blessed Angels and Saints of God, pray for me, a poor sinner, that I may repent from my evil ways, that my heart may henceforth be forever united with yours in eternal love.

Amen.

PRAYER BEFORE
CONFESSION

I, a great sinner, come before you Lord, acknowledging my many sins and with an earnest desire to repent and to sin no more.

Grant me perfect contrition for my sins, that I may detest them with deep sorrow.

Send forth Your light into my soul and reveal to me all those sins which I ought to confess at this time.

Assist me with Your grace that I may be sincere and humble in confessing them.

O Mary, my mother, be with me and help me to obtain remission of my sins with a contrite heart.

Amen

INVOCATION TO THE HOLY SPIRIT BEFORE CONFESSION

O Holy Spirit, Source of all Light and Mercy, Spirit of Divine Wisdom, of Understanding and of Knowledge, come to my assistance and help me to make a good confession.

Enlighten me and help me to know my sins as one day I will have to recognise them before Your judgment seat.

Bring to my mind the evil which I have done and the good which I have neglected.

Permit me not to be blinded by self love and pride. Grant me heartfelt sorrow for my transgressions and the grace of a sincere confession, so that I may be forgiven and admitted again into Your friendship.

Amen.

RECEIVE MY CONFESSION

*R*eceive my confession, O most loving Saviour, Our Lord Jesus Christ, my only hope for the salvation of my soul. Grant me true contrition of my sins, so that day and night I will atone for my many sins.

Light of the world, You gave Yourself up to death on the Cross, to save me, a sinner; look upon me and have pity on me and give me the light to know my sins, true sorrow for my sins and a firm purpose of never committing them again.

O gracious Virgin Mary, Immaculate Mother of Jesus, I implore you to obtain for me by your powerful intercession these graces from your Divine Son.

St. Joseph, pray for me.

Amen

ST. LEONARD'S PRAYER BEFORE CONFESSION

O most loving Trinity, Father, Son and Holy Spirit, my God, I adore You. Behold this wretched creature at Your feet, who desires to make his peace with You by means of a good Confession.

But since, O my God, without Your help, I can do nothing but evil, I implore You, from Your Merciful Heart, grant me light, that I may recollect all my sins; make me realise the enormity of sin, so that I may detest it with all my heart.

O my Jesus, Fountain of Mercy, I draw near You that You may wash and cleanse me of my sin.

O Sun of justice, illuminate this poor blind creature.

O Divine Physician, heal this poor sick man.

O infinite Love, inflame this soul with Your love, so that it may break down and dissolve in tears of grief.

And may this confession be such that I may now in earnest change my life and never again find myself separated from You, my God, my hope, my love, the salvation, life, and peace of my poor soul!

Amen

"Two men went to the temple to pray. One was a Pharisee, the other one was a tax collector.

The Pharisee stood up and said this prayer "God, I thank You because I am not like the rest of these people, robbers, cheats, adulterers, or even like this tax collector. I fast twice a week and I pay a tenth of all I have."

But the tax collector, standing at a distance, would not even raise his eyes towards Heaven, but struck his chest and said:

God, be merciful to me, a sinner"

(Luke 18:10-13)

The prayer that comes from
the heart with true contrition
is the key that opens the
Merciful Heart of God.

Prescribed prayers are there only to help
you when you cannot think
of what to say to God,
but even better is to simply talk to God
in your own sincere way.

Talking to God is the best prayer and
gives us our own personal
relationship with Him.

Acts of Contrition

My Merciful God!

O my Merciful God, I acknowledge that my sins are many and grievous. But if I committed only one, in committing it, I have offended Your infinite perfection.

Why is my heart not penetrated with infinite grief and regret? I have sinned against Your goodness, which I should have loved more than anything else.

I preferred a petty honour, some vain interest, a miserable pleasure to Your Sovereign Majesty, which I should have adored, served and honoured.

My God, have mercy and forgive my sins. Infinite Goodness, how did I have the courage to offend You and to despise Your Will?

Now, I heartily repent of all my ingratitude and disloyalty. I wish sincerely that I had

never offended You and I resolve never to offend You again!

I would rather sacrifice all that I have than ever more to offend You.

O Mary, Mother of Mercy, take me under your protection and do not permit me ever more to rebel against God.

Reflection on the injury done to God by Sin

Think of the extreme injury sin does to God. On the one side, set before you the benefit of sin, which is the pleasure you expect to receive by it; on the other side, consider the offence you commit against God, which makes you lose His Friendship.

Then you put in balance God and your pleasure and you decide to lose the favour and friendship of God rather than your fleeting pleasure.

Can anything be more striking or can any greater affront to God be imagined than to prefer our sin before Him?

This imitates the madness of the crowd who, being offered their choice of Jesus or Barabbas, preferred the robber rather than Jesus Christ.

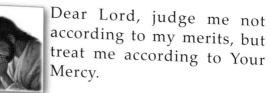 Dear Lord, judge me not according to my merits, but treat me according to Your Mercy.

Give me light, give me sorrow for the offences which I have committed against You and forgive me!

Merciful Heart of Jesus, have mercy on me. Mary, Mother of Mercy, intercede for me to obtain the grace to love Jesus Christ and never more to offend Him!

Reflection on the presence of God, before whom sin is committed

Think that the Most Blessed Trinity, Father, Son and the Holy Spirit, the only and almighty God is everywhere present, knows all things and penetrates the innermost and most secret thoughts of our heart.

He is that Divine and Infinite Mercy and Majesty, before Whom the highest Seraphim tremble with a holy fear and veil their faces through respect...and we have the courage to sin in His presence...

We have the courage to think, to say and to do things that would cover us with shame in front of other people. Still, we choose to do all this in His presence.

Reflect moreover that God, before Whom we commit sin, is our Judge, Who, at the moment of our death, will inevitably pass

the   sentence   upon   our thoughts, words and actions of which we may be found guilty.

Lord, give me the courage to come back to You and in Your Divine Presence, to confess my sins and to obtain Your Divine Mercy and the strength I need to stay always in Your Light.

Have Mercy on Me

Supreme and Merciful God, You Who know and see all things, even those secrets that pass in the interior of my heart, unknown by anyone else, is it possible that I dare to appear in Your presence, after having been so unfaithful to You?

I cannot run from You, because You are present everywhere; I cannot hide myself from You, because You see all things!

O my God, have mercy on me! I detest with all my heart all my sins, and I trust in Your unfathomable Love and Mercy!

Amen

The Paths of Repentance

by St. John Chrysostom - Doctor of the Church

Would you like me to tell you about the paths of repentance? They are numerous and quite varied and all lead to heaven.

A first path of repentance is to condemn your own sins. You should be the first to admit your sins and you will be justified. It was for this reason, too, that the prophet wrote: "I said: I will accuse myself of my sins to the Lord and you forgave the wickedness of my heart."

*T*herefore, you should con-demn your own sins, too; this will be enough reason for the Lord to forgive you, because a man who condemns his own sins is slower to commit them again. Rouse your conscience to accuse you, within your own heart, lest it becomes your accuser before the judgment seat of God. This is then one very good path of repentance.

*A*nother one and by no means a less valuable one is to put out of our minds the harm done us by our enemies, in order to control our anger and to have mercy and to forgive those who sinned against us. Then our own sins against the Lord will be forgiven us.

*F*ollowing this path, you will have another way to atone for sin: for if you forgive your debtors, your Father in Heaven will forgive you.

*D*o you want to know of a third path? It is that of prayer that is fervent, careful and comes from your heart.

*I*f you want to hear of a fourth, I will mention almsgiving and deeds of mercy, whose power is great and far-reaching.

*I*f, again, a man chooses to live a modest and humble life, that, no less than the other things I have mentioned, takes sin away. The proof of this you will find in the Bible, as the tax-collector who had no good deeds to mention, but offered his humility instead, and was relieved of the heavy burden of his sins.

*T*hus I have shown you five paths of repentance; condemnation of your own sins, forgiveness of our neighbours' sins against us, prayer, almsgiving and humility.

*D*o not be idle, then, but live daily and walk daily in all these paths; they are easy and you cannot plead your poverty. For, though you live out your life amid greatest need, you can always set aside your wrath, you can always be humble, pray diligently and condemn your own sins; poverty is no hindrance.

Poverty therefore is not an obstacle to carry out the Lord's bidding, even when it comes to that path of repentance which involves giving money (almsgiving, I mean). The widow proved that when she put her two coins into the box!

Now that we have learned how to heal these wounds of ours, let us apply the cures. Then when we have regained genuine health, we can approach the holy table with confidence and trust, we can go gloriously to meet Christ, the King of glory and all mercies and attain the eternal blessings through the grace, mercy and kindness of Jesus Christ, our Lord.

Prayers

after

Confession

A PRAYER AFTER CONFESSION

Almighty God and merciful Lord, once again You have shown me Your infinite mercy by accepting me back even though I have gone away from You, and lived my own way.

I renounce with my whole heart all the sins of my past life and resolve to commit them no more. I promise to abhor sin and to avoid all the occasions that lead to it.

Lord, I know that without You I can do nothing therefore, trusting in Your grace I want to begin a new life.

Mary, Mother of Mercy and my mother, be at my side and assist me always!

Amen

A SIMPLE PRAYER AFTER
CONFESSION

*D*ear Jesus, my Merciful Lord, thank You for helping me to make a good Confession, and thank You for taking away my sins.

Help me, dear Jesus, never to offend You again!

Mary, Mother of Mercy and my mother, pray to Jesus for me!

My dear Guardian Angel, help me and guide me always!

A PRATER OF HOPE
AFTER CONFESSION

My God and my Lord, today, by the merits of Your Sacrifice on the Cross, I hope that I have been pardoned. I thank You above all things. I hope one day to reach heaven, where I shall praise Your mercies forever. My God, I have lost Your grace so often, I now desire to lose You no more!

From this day forward I will change my life in earnest. You alone deserve all my love; I will love You with all my heart and I will no longer see myself separated from You.

I have promised You this already; now I repeat my promise of being ready to die rather than offend You again.

I promise also to avoid all occasions of sin, and to use such means as will prevent me from falling again.

 My Jesus, You know my weakness: give me grace to be faithful to You until death, and to have recourse to You when I am tempted.

My most holy mother, Mary, help me! You are the Mother of Mercy and perseverance, pray for me!

Jesus, I place all my trust in You!

THANKSGIVING AFTER
CONFESSION

*E*ternal Father and my Merciful Saviour, I thank You for Your goodness and mercy!

You had compassion on me, although in my folly I had wandered far away from You and offended You most grievously.

With a Father's love, You have received me anew after so many relapses into sin and forgiven me my offences through the holy sacrament of Penance.

Blessed be forever, O my God, Your loving kindness and Your infinite mercy! I pray that never again will I grieve You by ingratitude, by disobedience to Your holy will.

All that I am, all that I have, all that I do shall be consecrated to Your service and Your glory!

Amen.

Jesus I Trust in You

DIVINE MERCY AND THE SACRAMENT OF CONFESSION

Confession is the greatest way to experience God's Mercy!

Do not fear going to confession:

Most people today have difficulties with going to confession. Sometimes it is the lack of understanding, sometimes a sense of uneasiness or fear that keeps people away, often for years and years on end. Remember what Jesus said to St. Faustina: "Speak to the world about My Mercy." (D.848) Over and over again, Jesus expressed His desire that the whole world would come to the Fount of His Mercy:

"The greater the sinner, the greater the Mercy (...) The well of Mercy was opened wide with a lance on the Cross, for all souls. I do not exclude anyone" (Diary of St.Faustina)

So it comes as no surprise that Divine Mercy as a devotion is bringing more and more people back to this Sacrament, for no devotion in the history of Christianity put so much emphasis on the Mercy of God!

Once we understand that **now is the time for mercy**, our path towards reconciliation is widely open and available to anyone. And so important is this Holy Sacrament in the eyes of God, that Jesus Himself, in the message on His Divine Mercy, attached most wonderful promises to it, as part of the preparation for another wonderful gift to humanity, the Feast of Mercy (a Feast rightly compared by theologians to a second baptism): "The soul that will go to confession and receive Holy Communion shall obtain complete forgiveness of all sins and punishment" (II.138)

(A complete explanation with prayers, novena, the Feast of Mercy, conditions for obtaining the gift of Mercy and all other aspects of the

*Devotion are available in the book "Will You Help Me" - The Handbook of Devotion to the Divine Mercy, a book that has sold more than **4 million copies** and continues to sell in thousands helping to save lives and souls - see last page of this book.)*

Thinking of it, from a human point of view, the sacrament of Reconciliation is truly a divine miracle. A priest explained this once in a great way, saying that first of all, for such a Sacrament to exist, two things are needed: a penitent and a confessor. From a human perspective, he said, if you are away from God, just think how difficult it is to take a human being, with all his pride, burdened with guilt, fears and worries, and ask him to kneel down in front of another human being and to open up his heart, confessing things that he is hiding not only from people around him, but even from himself!

But this is not all: if "creating" a penitent was indeed difficult, how difficult would it

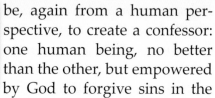 be, again from a human perspective, to create a confessor: one human being, no better than the other, but empowered by God to forgive sins in the name of God, his heart trained to heal wounds and his lips sealed forever in the Sacrament of Confession, that whatever was said "with God as witness", would never be revealed again on this earth...

Impossible to create from a human perspective, this sacrament exists because of God's Mercy for humankind and the link between "penitent-confessor" is actually a wonderful gift and a reality; and from such a great mystery, miracle and Sacrament flows the supernatural peace and forgiveness that only God can give, and give it freely and abundantly!

Indeed, such a Sacrament would only be possible if created by God!

If fears and scruples keep you away from this Sacrament, remember that priests today are a lot more under-standing and sympathetic to those fears, so do not hesitate to make them known to the priest and he will help you. He  is there to help and guide you, if asked.

Remember that it is not judgment awaiting in confessional, but spiritual healing and peace.

Jesus said to Saint Faustina:

"When you go to confession, know this, that I am waiting for you in the confessional. I am only hidden by the priest, but I myself act in the soul. Here the misery of the soul meets the God of Mercy. From this fount of Mercy souls draw graces solely with the vessel of trust. If their trust is great there is no limit to My generosity". (Diary VI 6-7).

"Every time you go to confession, immerse yourself entirely in My Mercy, with great trust, so that I may pour the bounty of My grace upon your soul. When you approach the confessional, know this, that I Myself am waiting there for you." (1602)

"Write, speak of My mercy. Tell souls where they are to look for solace; that is, in the Tribunal of Mercy (the Sacrament of Reconciliation).

There the greatest miracles take place and are incessantly repeated. (...) It suffices to come with faith to the feet of My representative and to reveal to him one's misery, and the miracle of Divine Mercy will be fully demonstrated." (1448)

Pray for souls that they be not afraid to approach the Tribunal of My Mercy. Do not grow weary of praying for sinners" (975)

"My daughter, tell him (the priest) everything and reveal your soul to him as you do before Me. Do not fear anything. It is to keep you in peace  that I place this priest between your soul and Myself.

The words he will speak to you are My words. Reveal to him your soul's greatest secrets. I will give him light to know your soul." (232)

PRAYERS
EVERY CATHOLIC
SHOULD KNOW

THE HOLY ROSARY

The Holy Rosary is composed of twenty decades, each decade consisting of the Our Father, the Hail Mary, and the Glory be to the Father; and each being recited in honour of some mystery in the life of Our Lord and of His Blessed Mother.

During each decade, we should call to mind the mystery which it is intended to honour, and pray that we may learn to practise the virtue specially taught us by that mystery.

A plenary indulgence may be gained, under the usual conditions for the recitation of the Rosary (five decades are sufficient), in a church or public oratory or in the family. If the Rosary is said privately a partial indulgence may be gained:

THE FIVE JOYFUL MYSTERIES
1. The Annunciation. *(Luke 1.26-38)*
2. The Visitation. *(Luke 1.39-50)*
3. The Birth of Our Lord. *(Luke 1.14)*
4. The Presentation in the Temple. *(Luke 2.22-35)*
5. The Finding of Jesus in the Temple. *(Luke 2.42-52)*

THE FIVE SORROWFUL MYSTERIES
1. The Agony in the Garden. *(Matt.26.36-46)*
2. The Scourging at the Pillar. *(Matt.27.17-26)*
3. The Crowning with Thorns. *(Matt.27.27-30)*
4. The Carrying of the Cross. *(Matt.27. 31-32)*
5. The Crucifixion. *(John 19.17-42)*

THE FIVE GLORIOUS MYSTERIES
1. The Resurrection. *(Matt.28.1-8)*
2. Ascension of Christ into Heaven. *(Acts 1.6-11)*
3. The Descent of the Holy Spirit. *(Acts 2.1-13)*
4. The Assumption. *(Redemptoris Mater)*
5. Coronation of the Virgin Mary. *(Rev. 12.1-2)*

THE FIVE LUMINOUS MYSTERIES
1. The Baptism of Jesus in the Jordan. *(Matt.3.13)*
2. The Wedding at Cana. *(Jn. 2.1-12)*
3. Jesus Proclaims the Kingdom. *(Matt.1.15, 2.3-13)*
4. Jesus' Transfiguration. *(Luke. 9. 34)*
5. Institution of the Eucharist. *(Jn. 6. 22- 65)*

Then is said:

Hail, Holy Queen, Mother of Mercy; hail our
life, our sweetness and our hope. To you do we
cry, poor banished children of Eve; to you do
we send up our sighs, mourning and weeping
in this valley of tears. Turn then, most gracious
advocate, your eyes of mercy towards us and

after this our exile, show unto us the blessed fruit of your womb, Jesus.

O clement, O loving, O sweet Virgin Mary.
V. Pray for us O Holy Mother of God.

R. That we may be made worthy of the promises of Christ.

Let us pray,

O God, whose only begotten Son, by His life, death and resurrection, has purchased for us the rewards of eternal life; grant, we beseech You, that while meditating on these mysteries of the most holy Rosary of the Blessed Virgin Mary, we may imitate what they contain, and obtain what they promise, through the same Christ Our Lord.

Amen.

THE FIFTEEN PROMISES OF MARY TO CHRISTIANS WHO RECITE THE ROSARY

1. Whoever shall faithfully serve me by the recitation of the Rosary, shall receive signal graces.

2. I promise my special protection and the greatest graces to all those who shall recite the Rosary.

3. The Rosary shall be a powerful armour against hell, it will destroy vice, decrease sin, and defeat heresies.

4. It will cause virtue and good works to flourish: it will obtain for souls the abundant mercy of God; it will withdraw the hearts of people from the love of the world and its vanities, and will lift them to the desire of eternal things. Oh that souls would sanctify themselves by these means.

5. The soul which recommends itself to me by the recitation of the Rosary, shall not perish.

6. Whoever shall recite the Rosary devoutly, applying themselves to the consideration of its sacred mysteries shall never be conquered by misfortune. God will not chastise them in His justice, they shall not perish by an unprovided death; if they be just they shall remain in the grace of God, and become worthy of eternal life.

7. Whoever shall have a true devotion for the Rosary shall not die without the sacraments of the Church.

8. Those who are faithful to recite the Rosary shall have during their life and at their death the light of God and the plenitude of His graces; at the moment of death they shall participate in the merits of the saints in paradise.

9. I shall deliver from purgatory those who have been devoted to the Rosary.

10. The faithful children of the Rosary shall merit a high degree of glory in heaven.

11. You shall obtain all you ask of me by the recitation of the Rosary.

12. All those who propagate the holy Rosary shall be aided by me in their necessities.

13. I have obtained from my Divine Son that all the advocates of the Rosary shall have for intercessors the entire celestial court during their life and at the hour of death.

14. All those who recite the Rosary are my sons and daughters and children of my only son Jesus Christ.

15. Devotion to my Rosary is a great sign of predestination.

(Given to St. Dominic)

THE APOSTLES CREED

I believe in God, the Father Almighty, Creator of Heaven and Earth, and in Jesus Christ, His only Son, our Lord, Who was conceived by the Holy Spirit, born of the Virgin Mary, suffered under Pontius Pilate, was crucified, died, and was buried. He descended into Hell. The third day he rose again from the dead; He ascended into Heaven, and is seated at the right hand of God the Father Almighty. From thence He shall come to judge the living and the dead. I believe in the Holy Spirit, the holy Catholic Church the communion of saints, the forgiveness of sins, the resurrection of the body, and life everlasting. Amen.

THE CONFITEOR

I confess to almighty God and to you, my brothers and sisters, that I have greatly sinned in my thoughts and in my words, in what I have done and in what I have failed to do, through my fault, through my fault, through my most grievous fault; therefore I ask blessed Mary ever-Virgin, all the Angels and Saints, and you, my brothers and sisters, to pray for me to the Lord our God.

SHORT ACT OF CONTRITION

O my God, because You are so good, I am very sorry that I have sinned against You and by the help of Your grace I will not sin again.

May be said at morning, noon or night, to put us in mind that God the Son became man for our salvation.

V. The Angel of the Lord declared unto Mary:
R. And she conceived of the Holy Spirit.
Hail Mary etc.

V. Behold the handmaid of the Lord:
R. Be it done unto me according to Your word.
Hail Mary etc.

V. And the Word was made Flesh:
R. And dwelt among us. *Hail Mary etc.*

V. Pray for us O holy Mother of God.
R. That we may be made worthy of the promises of Christ.

Let us pray

Pour forth, we beseech You, O Lord, Your grace into our hearts, that, we, to whom the incarnation of Christ, Your Son, was made known by the message of an angel, may, by His Passion and Cross, be brought to the glory of His Resurrection, through the same Christ, Our Lord.

R. Amen.

May the divine assistance remain always with us

and may the souls of the faithful departed, through the mercy of God, rest in peace.

R. Amen

The Regina Caeli is a prayer that replaces the Angelus during the Easter Season from Holy Saturday to the Saturday after Pentecost. The prayer is included in the Enchiridion of Indulgences.

REGINA CAELI

Queen of heaven, rejoice, alleluia:
For He whom you merited to bear, alleluia,
Has risen, as he said, alleluia.

Pray for us to God, alleluia.

V. Rejoice and be glad, O Virgin Mary, alleluia.

R. Because the Lord is truly risen, alleluia.

Let Us Pray.

O God, Who by the Resurrection of Your Son, our Lord Jesus Christ, granted joy to the whole world, grant, we beg You, that through the intercession of the Virgin Mary, His Mother, we may lay hold of the joys of eternal life.

Through the same Christ our Lord.

R. Amen.

THE MEMORARE

Remember, O most gracious Virgin Mary, that never was it known, that anyone who fled to your protection, implored your help or sought your intercession, was left unaided. Inspired with this confidence I fly to You, O Virgin of Virgins, my Mother.

To you I come, before you I stand, sinful and sorrowful. O Mother of the word incarnate, despise not my petition, but in Your mercy, hear and answer me. Amen.

PRAYER TO SAINT MICHAEL

Saint Michael the Archangel, defend us in our hour of need; be our safeguard against the wickedness and snares of the devil; may God restrain him, we humbly pray; and do thou, O Prince of the Heavenly Host, by the Power of God, thrust Satan into hell and with him all evil spirits, who wander through the world for the ruin of souls. Amen.

PRAYER FOR GUIDANCE
TO THE HOLY SPIRIT

Come Holy Spirit, Spirit of infinite Holiness,
Spirit of infinite Wisdom,
Spirit of infinite Truth, impart to us,
Thoughts higher than our own thoughts,
Prayers deeper than our own prayers,
Wisdom beyond our own wisdom,
so that under Your Divine influence we may
always choose the ways of truthfulness,
goodness and love, after the perfect image
of Our Lord and Saviour Jesus Christ, Amen.

THE CHAPLET OF DIVINE MERCY

Jesus said to Saint Faustina: **"Say unceasingly this chaplet that I have taught you. Anyone who says it will receive great Mercy at the hour of death. Priests will recommend it to sinners as the last hope. Even the most hardened sinner, if he recites this Chaplet even once, will receive grace from my infinite Mercy. I want the whole world to know My Infinite Mercy. I want to give unimaginable graces to those who trust in My Mercy"**.

This Chaplet can be said on ordinary Rosary beads:

First say, one **Our Father**, one **Hail Mary** and the **I believe in God**.

Then on the large beads say the following words:

Eternal Father, I offer You the Body and Blood, Soul and Divinity of Your dearly beloved Son Our Lord Jesus Christ, in atonement for our sins and those of the whole world.

On the smaller beads you are to say
the following prayer:

**For the sake of His sorrowful Passion
have mercy on us and
on the whole world.**

After the five decades you are to say
this prayer three times.

**Holy God, Holy Mighty One,
Holy Immortal One,
have mercy on us
and on the whole world**

My daughter, try your best to make the stations of the Cross in this hour, provided that your duties permit it; and if you are not able to make the Stations of the Cross, then at least step into the chapel, for a moment and adore, in the Most Blessed Sacrament, My Heart which is full of mercy, and should you be unable to step into the chapel immerse yourself in prayer, wherever you happen to be, if only for a very brief instant".

SUGGESTED THREE O'CLOCK PRAYERS

*At this hour you can obtain everything
for yourself and for others*

Beg Jesus, at this hour (the hour of 3 o'clock) to have mercy on all the poor souls who are about to die and are on their way to eternal damnation. No greater act of mercy, can you pray for.

Prayer

You expired, Jesus, but the source of life gushed forth for souls and an ocean of mercy opened up for the whole world. O Fount of Life, unfathomable Divine Mercy, envelop the whole world and empty Yourself out upon us. (D. 1319)

This prayer was given to Saint Faustina as a conversion prayer, (see Divine Mercy Handbook of Devotion) and it has been adopted as an appropriate short prayer for 3 o'clock. The following is the prayer given by Jesus to St. Faustina:

"O Blood and Water, which gushed forth from the Heart of Jesus as a fount of mercy for us, I trust in You."

BASIC CHRISTIAN DOCTRINE

THE TEN COMMANDMENTS OF GOD

1. I am the Lord your God and you shall not have strange Gods before Me.
2. You shall not take the name of the Lord your God in vain.
3. Remember that you keep holy the Sabbath day. *(in the Christian Church Sunday).*
4. Honour your father and your mother.
5. You shall not kill.
6. You shall not commit adultery.
7. You shall not steal.
8. You shall not bear false witness against your neighbour.
9. You shall not covet (desire) your neighbour's wife.
10. You shall not covet (desire) your neighbour's goods.

PRECEPTS OF THE CHURCH

1. To keep the Sundays and Holy days of Obligation holy, by hearing Mass and resting from servile works.
2. To keep the days of Fasting and Abstinence appointed by the Church.
3. To go to Confession at least once a year.

4. To receive the Blessed Sacrament at least once a year, at Easter or thereabouts.

5. To contribute to the support of your priests.

6. Not to marry within certain degrees of kindred without dispensation.

THE SEVEN SACRAMENTS

1. **Baptism**: by which we are made Christians; children of God, members of His holy Church and heirs to the kingdom of Heaven.

2. **Confirmation:** by which we receive the Holy Spirit, to make us strong Christians and imbue us with the Spirit of Mercy

3. **The Holy Eucharist:** which is really and truly and substantially the Body and Blood, the Soul and Divinity of Jesus Christ under the appearances of bread and wine. The Holy Eucharist is not only a Sacrament, in which we receive our Divine Lord for the food and nourishment of our souls, and in which He is really present to be adored upon the altar; it is also a sacrifice, the Sacrifice of the Holy Mass, in which, at the time of consecration, the bread and

wine are changed into the Body and Blood of Jesus Christ, and in which He is offered up for us to His Eternal Father.

4. **Penance:** by which the sins committed after Baptism are forgiven, and one of the greatest sources of God's mercy.

5. **Anointing of the Sick:** which, in dangerous illness, and in preparation for death, comforts the soul, remits sin, and restores health if God sees this to be expedient.

6. **Holy Orders**: by which Bishops, Priests and other Ministers of the Church receive power and grace to perform their sacred duties.

7. **Matrimony:** which is the Sacrament of Christian Marriage.

THE SEVEN DEATHLY SINS

Pride
Covetousness
Lust
Anger
Gluttony
Envy
Sloth

The Three Theological Virtues:
Faith, Hope and Charity.

The Four Cardinal Virtues:
Prudence, Justice, Fortitude, Temperance,

The Seven Gifts of the Holy Spirit:
Wisdom, Understanding, Counsel, Piety,
Fortitude, Knowledge, Fear of the Lord.

The Twelve Fruits of the Holy Spirit:
Charity, Joy, Peace, Patience, Kindness,
Goodness, Forbearance, Mildness, Faith,
Modesty, Self restraint, Chastity.

The Seven Corporal Works of Mercy:
To feed the hungry; to give drink to the thirsty;
to clothe the naked; to help the homeless; to
visit the sick; to visit the imprisoned;
to bury the dead.

The Seven Spiritual Works of Mercy:
Admonish sinners; instruct the uninformed;
counsel the doubtful; comfort the sorrowful;
be patient with those in error; forgive offenses;
pray for the living and the dead.

IMPORTANT DATES IN CHURCH CALENDAR

Advent: begins on the Sunday nearest the 30th November, it is in preparation for Christmas, or the coming of Our Lord. Advent has four Sundays.

Christmas: which celebrates the Birth of Our Lord, begins at the Christmas Vigil on the eve of Christmas and ends on the 6th January, the celebration of the Baptism of Our Lord.

Lent: this is a time in preparation for Easter, and begins on Ash Wednesday and ends with the Easter Vigil. Passion Sunday or Palm Sunday: this is the sixth Sunday of Lent and is the beginning of Holy Week.

Easter Vigil: this is on Easter Saturday night when the Church awaits the Resurrection of Christ.

Easter: this is the most important time in the Church year, when we remember the Passion, Death and Resurrection of Jesus Christ. It is known as the Easter Triduum. It begins with the evening Mass on Holy Thursday, and finishes with the evening prayers on Easter Sunday

Feast of Mercy: first Sunday after Easter. The Feast has been called "a second baptism", where a complete cleansing of our immortal soul can be obtained, if one complies with all the conditions requested by Our Lord (declared a solemn feast day by John Paul II)

The Ascension: is usually celebrated on the fortieth day after Easter.

Pentecost: celebrated fifty days after Easter to commemorate the descent of the Holy Spirit on the Apostles. It is also considered the birth of the Church.

Trinity Sunday: this is the Sunday after Pentecost, and celebrates the mystery of the Father, the Son and the Holy Spirit.

Corpus Christi: is the Thursday after Trinity Sunday, and celebrates the Body and Blood of Christ.

Fast and Abstinence: Ash Wednesday and Good Friday are the only two official fast days of the Church, although today the Church encourages us to fast more often, especially on Fridays, the day of Our Lord's Passion. This is the day when self-denial should be practiced. The form of self-denial, to be offered in union with Our Lord's suffering on the Cross, is left to the free choice of each individual. The age at which abstinence becomes binding is fourteen.

The obligation of fasting is restricted to those who have completed their eighteenth year until they have begun their sixtieth. Since November 21st, 1964, the following rules apply at whatever time of day Holy Communion is received:

1. Water may be taken at any time.

2. Solid food and drinks may be taken up to one hour before Holy Communion.

3. The sick (not necessarily bed-ridden) may also take genuine medicines, solid or liquid as well as non-alcoholic drinks at any time before Communion. The fast from solid food and drink is about a quarter of an hour for the sick and aged and those attending them.

FEAST DAYS

Jan. 1.	Mary, the Mother of God
Jan. 6.	Epiphany
Jan. 25.	Conversion of St. Paul
Jan. 28.	St. Thomas Aquinas

Feb. 2.	Presentation of Jesus
Feb. 22.	St. Peter, first Pope

Mar. 8.	St. John of God
Mar. 17.	St. Patrick
Mar. 19.	St. Joseph, the husband of Mary
Mar. 25.	Annunciation by the Angel Gabriel to Mary

Apr. 25.	St. Mark the Evangelist

May 1.	St. Joseph the Worker
May 3.	St. Philip and St. James, Apostles
May 13.	Our Lady of Fatima
May 14.	St. Matthias, Apostle
May 31.	Visitation by Mary to Elizabeth

June 11.	St. Barnabas, Apostle
June 13.	St. Anthony of Padua
June 24.	Birth of St. John the Baptist
June 29.	St. Peter and St. Paul, Apostles

July 3.	St. Thomas, Apostle

July 16.	Our Lady of Mount Carmel
July 22.	St. Mary Magdalene
July 25.	St. James, Apostle
July 31.	St. Ignatius Loyola

Aug. 6.	The Transfiguration
Aug. 8.	St. Dominic
Aug. 11.	St. Clare
Aug. 15.	Assumption of Mary to Heaven
Aug. 22.	Queenship of Mary
Aug. 24.	St. Barthlomew, Apostle
Aug. 29.	Beheading of St. John the Baptist

Sept. 8.	Birthday of Mary
Sept. 14.	Triumph of the Cross
Sept. 15.	Our Lady of Sorrows
Sept. 21.	St. Matthew, Apostle
Sept. 27.	St. Vincent de Paul
Sept. 29.	Archangels Michael, Gabriel and Raphael

Oct. 1.	St. Theresa of the Child Jesus
Oct. 2.	Guardian Angels
Oct. 4.	St. Francis of Assisi
Oct. 5.	Saint Faustina
Oct. 7.	Our Lady of the Rosary
Oct. 18.	St. Luke, Evangelist
Oct. 28.	St. Simon and St. Jude, Apostles

Nov. 1.   All Saints
Nov. 2.   All Souls
Nov. 3.   St. Martin De Porres
Nov. 21. Presentation of Mary
Nov. 30. St. Andrew, Apostle

Dec. 3.   Francis Xavier
Dec. 8.   Immaculate Conception
Dec. 21.   Peter Canisius
Dec. 25.   Christmas, the birth of Jesus
Dec. 26.   St. Stephen
Dec. 27.   John, Apostle and Evangelist
Dec. 28.   Holy Innocents

*Sunday After Easter:
(Feast of Divine Mercy)

"A soul does not benefit as it should from the sacrament of confession if it is not humble. Pride keeps it in darkness. The soul neither knows how, nor is it willing, to probe with precision the depths of its own misery. It puts on a mask and avoids everything that might bring it recovery."

(St.Faustina's Diary - 113)

Did you know that...

No book on Confession would be complete without mentioning two great Saints who contributed greatly to the salvation of many souls in their own time while on earth and continue to intercede for many as Saints in heaven.

St. John Vianney served as a humble parish priest in the little village of Ars, in France, but his great zeal in caring for lost souls and his gift of discernment, prophecy, and hidden knowledge brought thousands to his confessional. There, he spent long hours showing mercy and patience and helping to lift the burden from people's souls.

He is honoured now as the patron Saint of parish priests and his humility and profound knowledge of God's Mercy are a great inspiration for every generation of priests.

Beside St. John Vianney, St. Philip Neri, (born in Italy in the 16th century) is also known for his zeal in hearing confessions and bringing many souls back to God.

His work among the poor and the sick in Rome allowed him to know the depth of human suffering and to have great compassion on human souls.

He spent his last day of his life in confessional and throughout his life, he looked at this Sacrament of the Church with great reverence and responsibility.

"...FOR HE WAS DEAD AND HAS COME BACK TO LIFE..."

A TRUE DEATH-ROW STORY

The following is the true story of Brent Gardner, a prisoner on death row in an American prison.

Brent Gardner was a labouring man who worked on a farm. He had got married when he was 17 years old to a woman of the same age.

He never had much education and left school when he was fourteen years old. He was not great with words and when he got into an argument usually ended up using his fists to win the debate.

One night a couple of drunks made a remark about his wife, Brent flew into a rage, broke a bottle on the edge of the bar and slashed the throats of the two men.

Brent was arrested and charged with

murder, he was found guilty and was placed in a cell on death row having been sentenced to die. Awaiting execu-  tion, he shared a cell with Otis, another death row prisoner with whom he became friends.

On the final night of Otis' life he was preparing himself to go to his death by prayer and reading the Bible. The next morning Brent found the man completely at peace and in good humour. Brent wondered how he himself would face the day of his execution. He asked Otis why he did not fear death. He answered "because I have repented, made a good confession and I am ready to go to a better place..." Brent said "you believe in God then?"

The man said "...well... I didn't, until a year ago when I was very ill in the prison hospital and on one occasion my mother visited the ward and put a medal around my neck. I was too weak to tell her to go away, that I didn't believe in that rubbish.

I found out later it was called a miraculous medal that she had put around my neck" Brent said, "I wish I had a mother... I never had a mother, she left home when I was too young to remember…"

"However…", Brent continued, "…you've got a medal that is miraculous?", and he started to laugh.

Otis said, "…you may laugh, but boy, was it miraculous for me, because I was back on my feet in a week…but the greatest miracle was that from then on, I believed and I'm now a confirmed Catholic. You know…it makes you strong and all your problems seem small and insignificant when you believe in God!"

"Now…" he said standing up, "…I won't want this medal any longer, so I'm giving it to you".

Brent hesitantly took it from him, but he insisted that Brent put it around his neck.

To Brent it was simply an ornament. But nevertheless he kept it around his neck.

A week later after his new friend was gone

to his eternity, Brent awakened one night and there beside his bed was the most beautiful woman he had ever seen.

At first he was very frightened, but the woman just said, "...you said you never had a mother but you always had, I am your Mother, your heavenly Mother".

With that, she disappeared as quickly as she had appeared.

Brent stayed awake all that night sitting up in bed, too afraid to sleep.

He decided to see a priest the next day and find out more about who this lady claimed to be. The priest explained that it was the Mother of God and in the Catholic religion it was believed she was the Mother of all mankind as well.

Brent was so taken aback he asked for

religious instruction, as he wanted to know more about this whole belief thing, as he put it himself.

Initially, the priest had difficulty believing this double murderer's story. When he went back to his parish, he told the Parish priest what this man had said he had seen and that he doubted him, could it be some kind of ruse.

The parish priest told him nevertheless it was his duty to give religious instruction, no matter who or where the request came from.

It was on his next meeting with Brent that the priest learned that Brent Gardner could neither read nor write. And his ignorance of religion was even more profound than he thought, he knew absolutely nothing.
Brent had to get instruction on how to read and write first before receiving religious instruction and to this end he began receiv-

ing help from other prisoners, who gave him a basic education in a very short period of time. Several months passed, and the time came when the priest was ready to give instructions to Brent about the Sacrament of Confession. The priest began with, "today I'm going to teach you about the Sacrament of Confession."

But Brent immediately stood up , before the priest could go any further, and said "I think I already know". "How could you know?" asked the priest. "Well..." said Brent "...the lady told me" .

"You have seen this lady again then?" said the priest, annoyed with this interruption at the beginning of his class.

"Yes, and she said that when we go to confession, we are kneeling down, not just before a priest, but we're kneeling down in the presence of Her Son...And that when we are truly sorry for our sins, the Blood and

138

Water that flowed from His side on the Cross flows down upon us and washes us free from all our sins, and renews our souls completely." The priest sat down stunned. Brent thought he was angry and said, "Don't be angry, I had to tell you what she said.." "I'm not angry..." said the priest, "...I'm just amazed, because I don't know where that statement comes from, for such a profound statement has to come from someone very knowledgeable about the Bible and also very spiritual."

Brent said, "she told me that if you doubted me or showed hesitancy in accepting what I say, then I was to remind you that you made a vow to her years ago which she's still waiting for you to keep."

The priest was astounded by this and had to ask "What was the vow then?", ready to call it a day if he heard some foolishness from Brent... but the priest could not believe his ears when Brent told him exactly what it was, and when it took place. The priest did not doubt Brent any longer and redoubled his efforts to instruct Brent on the catechism in order to prepare him for finally going to Confession.

The other prisoners were intrigued with Brent the-tough-guy's conversion. He kept telling them to go to confession, saying that "when you're in the confessional you're really talking to God, not a priest, we talk through the priest to God and God talks back to us through the priest."

About a week later, the priest was preparing to teach Brent about the Blessed Sacrament. Brent interrupted him once again and said "...the Lady told me about Holy Communion. She told me that I will see what looks like a piece of bread, but it is really and truly Her Son.

But the most important thing she told me was that when I received Jesus, He would be within me as He was with Her before He

"...Our Lady told me about Holy Communion, She told me that I will only see what looks like a piece of bread, but it is really and truly Her Son..."

was born in Bethlehem. And that I should spend my time like she did, adoring Him, thanking Him, praising Him and asking Him for blessings.

Then I would spend my last moments on earth entirely with Him!"

Brent was received into the Catholic Church that year, and then the time came for Brent to go. He was to be executed at five minutes after twelve, midnight.

After his last confession the priest asked him, "have you any last request before you die?"

Brent replied "what do you mean?...I'm not going to die...I'm just going to another life, my eternal life with my Mother in heaven."

Brent had requested the priest after his execution to have a Holy Hour for the rest of the prisoners.

The priest did not want to disillusion Brent

but he could not see any of the other hardened criminals coming to a holy hour, regardless of Brent's death-bed conversion.

However, in memory of Brent, he brought prayer books from the Church and started a Holy Hour, but did not bring the Blessed Sacrament.

The priest could not believe the number that turned up. He immediately went to the chapel and got the Blessed Sacrament. It was the most joyous holy hour he had ever experienced.

Afterwards many of the prisoners asked for religious instruction so that they too, could have this wonderful peace on their last day on earth.

"...the greater the sinner, the greater the mercy (...) for I desire to save all.

The well of Mercy was opened wide with a lance on the Cross, for all souls.

I do not exclude anyone."

(Jesus to St.Faustina)

*T*ell ailing mankind to draw
close to My Merciful Heart
and I will fill them with peace.

Mankind will not find

solace until it turns with

confidence to My Mercy."

(Jesus to St. Faustina)

Help Us Dry The Tears

("Divine Mercy in Action")

is a foundation started by
our Divine Mercy Publications Apostolate to help
bring the Message we spread, in deed as well as word
to as many poverty stricken children in countries
where there are no social services.

Sales of our publications fund this work but you
may also send
a donation to help:

"Help Us Dry The Tears"
a registered charity,
Charity No. CHY14320

You may send a donation directly
to Divine Mercy Publications
Maryville, Skerries, Co. Dublin, Ireland
please make cheques payable to
Help us dry the tears

or simply phone us at 01 849 1458 or
135 01 849 1458 from abroad to make a credit
card donation

Please visit - www.hudt.org

Since the collapse of communism in Eastern Europe thousands of children were left living in horrific conditions in the streets and sewers of these former socialist countries. And this is where we started helping these children, through our Foundation

"Help Us Dry The Tears" - HUDT

We opened **"Houses of Mercy"** in many Eastern European countries. We funded **life saving operations** for children in Marie Curie Children's Hospital in Bucharest.

We **paid for accommodation, food, heating, education for very poor families.** We opened a **medical clinic for the poor, an Educational Centre for children with long term illnesses.**

We built **two Divine Mercy Churches in Moldova** where there was no catholic church since 1945. **the first Hospice for the dying** in Lithuania, we also helped built a **Hospice for Terminally Ill Children.**

We built a **Divine Mercy Church in Georgia,** (old Soviet Union), we built **a Divine Mercy Church in Havana,** Cuba.

Churches because healing the poverty of the heavenly soul is more important than the poverty of the earthly body.

Our charity is motivated by our faith.